Stories for Feelings for children

Hilary Hawkes

Front cover credit and interior illustration:

selfpubbookcovers.com/DiversePixel

 Story Therapy®

Hello from Story Therapy®
We're a small, not-for-profits/voluntary project and member of Social Enterprise UK. Our resources aim to promote inclusion, friendship and understanding of ourselves and others. Our products are available to all, but we also donate our books and resources to groups, registered charities and organizations that help children's emotional growth and mental well-being. www.storytherapyresources.co.uk

Stories for Feelings

for children

Words © Hilary Hawkes

Front cover credit and interior illustration:
selfpubbookcovers.com/DiversePixel

First print edition by Strawberry Jam Books for Story Therapy® 2014

All rights reserved. No part of this publication may be reproduced, stored in a retrieval system, or transmitted in any form or by any means, electronic, mechanical, photocopying, recording or otherwise without the prior permission of Strawberry Jam Books. Hilary Hawkes has asserted her rights under the Copyright, Designs and Patents Act of 1988 to be identified as the author of this work.

British Library Cataloguing in Publication Data

A CIP catalogue record for this book is available from the British Library

Abingdon, UK

www.hilaryhawkes.co.uk/strawberryjambooks

ISBN 978-1-910257-09-8

The Tree.   page 5

Theme: Not comparing yourself to others negatively.

Being glad to be who you are.

Recognising your own qualities.

The Little Stream   page 10

Theme: Letting something go.

Allowing yourself to accept an ending of something and moving on.

Letting your life move on naturally.

A Heavy Load   page 15

Theme: Not carrying other people's worries or stuff.

Not getting worried about others.

Realising we're not meant to fix everyone or everything.

The Flower   page 22

Theme: Allowing change and growth in yourself.

Not being fearful.

Using your gifts, abilities.

Jack and the Rucksack   page 27

Not bottling things up inside.

Saying how you feel.

Knowing it's ok to ask for help.

The Wish   page 32

Dealing with feelings of exclusion that can be the result of being bullied.

Believing in yourself.

Having confidence to help yourself.

Broken   page 38

Not holding on to the past and putting the broken pieces of life back together.

Finding happiness and a way forward after something sad or bad has happened.

Acceptance.

The Tree

IT was autumn and the little oak tree stood in the middle of the woods with his brown and golden leaves.

The wind whooshed through the woods and made the little tree's branches swing and sway from side to side.

"It's great being the wind!" cried the wind. "I can blow high and low wherever I want! I'd be bored standing in one place all the time like you!"

The little tree thought about this. Was the wind right? Was it better to be able to blow high and low wherever you wanted instead of standing in one place all the time?

He just didn't know.

The sun shone down on the woods and warmed the air and made shadows dance on the woodland floor.

"It's great being the sun!" said the sun. "I can see all over the woods and all over the world from up here. It's much better being up here in the sky!"

The little tree thought about this. Was the sun right? Was it better to be up high in the blue sky looking down on everything else?

He just didn't know.

A squirrel leapt through the branches of the little tree looking for acorns.

"It's great being a squirrel!" chuckled the squirrel. "It's fun jumping through the trees collecting acorns for food for the baby squirrels. It's much better having something fun and important to do!"

The little tree thought about this. Was the squirrel right? Was it better to be able to jump through the trees finding acorns?

He just didn't know.

Time went by. The wind blew all the leaves off the little oak's branches. The sun shone high in the sky and the squirrels collected all the acorns. Autumn went and winter arrived. Snowflakes drifted gently across the woods and landed on the little oak.

"We're so pretty," sang the snowflakes. "We make everything look beautiful! It's much better being snow than a tree!"

Children arrived in the woods and made a snowman. They gave the snowman a big smiley face.

"It's great being a snowman!" grinned the snowman when the children had gone. "Everyone loves snow! It's much better being a snowman!"

The little tree thought about the snowflakes and the snowman. Were they right? Did everyone love the snow more than they loved the trees?

He just didn't know.

But he felt sad.

And he wished he wasn't a tree. It wasn't good enough.

Being anything else would be better.

Just then a shower of extra snow shook itself all over him from the big tree that stood next to him. Three wise owls sat in the big tree.

"What's up?" said the three wise owls.

The little tree sighed.

"It's no good being a tree," he said. "The wind and the sun and the squirrels and the snow are much better than me. They said so!"

"And you believed them?" asked the wise owls.

"Yes," said the little tree. "They get to blow wherever they want or see everything from high up or do fun and important things or be loved by everyone. I just stand here in one place."

"But you're a tree!" said the owls. "You're doing exactly what trees are supposed to do. You're not supposed to be the wind or the sun or a squirrel or a snowman. You don't need to be like them because you're not them. You're exactly right as you are!"

Just then a man wearing a thick jacket, scarf, gloves and boots traipsed through the woods right up to the little oak. He had a camera on a strap around his neck.

"Ah! Here it is!" he said out loud. Ignoring the snowman, he looked through the camera at the tree. The little tree looked beautiful against the clear winter sky. The wind swooshed the snow off some of his branches so that the beginnings of spring's new leaf buds could just be seen. Somewhere in the thicker branches the squirrels had made their safe winter house.

"Perfect!" said the man, clicking the camera several times. "A perfect oak tree!"

The little tree thought about this. Were the wise owls right? Was he exactly the way he was supposed to be? Was the man with the camera right? Was he really perfect for an oak tree?

The tree stood tall and proud. Yes, they were right. And he would grow into a big tree. The wind would blow, the sun would shine, the squirrels would leap and the snow would fall. But he, the oak tree, would stand sure and strong being exactly the way he was meant to be too.

He just knew it.

The Little Stream

THERE was once a bear who lived in a forest next to a sparkling, bubbling stream. The bear loved the sparkling, bubbling stream. It always seemed so happy and free as it bounced along over pebbles and stones and rocks.

Sometimes the bear played in the stream scooping up pawfuls of water and tossing them over his head. Other times he took long refreshing drinks from the stream. Other times he lay in the water and bathed, washing all the dust and mud from his fur.

It seemed to the bear that the stream was not only happy and free, but that it was also his friend. The bear loved the stream and looked forward to visiting it.

One hot day, as the bear played floating leaves along the stream, he noticed that there was less water than usual.

But the stream still sounded happy and free.

Then the next day when the bear scooped up a pawful of water for a cooling drink, his paw scraped the bottom of the stream. There was definitely less water than usual.

"No!" said the bear. "The stream is leaving me! It is flowing away! No! No! Please don't flow away. You are my friend!"

The bear was very sad. How could this be happening? What was he going to do without his friend? The bear sat down and cried. The stream was getting very shallow. Something was very wrong. The bear wiped his eyes with one big soft paw and decided to walk along the stream to see if he could find what was wrong.

It wasn't long before he came across the place where the stream started. This was where some water bubbled up from some rocks. It was a spring and it formed the little stream. But something was changing. For some reason less water was coming up from the rocks. Soon there would be no water. This wasn't fair, the bear thought. He needed the stream. It was his friend. Why didn't the stream want to be a stream any more?

The bear hurried back to where he liked to play in the water and began collecting stones and rocks and heavy logs. Then he placed the stones and rocks and heavy logs into the water so that they formed a dam across the stream. He filled in all the gaps with sticky mud and leaves and smaller rocks. Soon he had a good dam which the water in the flowing stream could not get past.

After all his hard work the bear lay down for a sleep. When he woke he stretched and yawned and listened for his friend. But he couldn't hear the happy free bubbling sound of the stream. He opened his eyes. He was pleased to see that the stream was very full of water again - because it couldn't get past the dam and flow away. It was so full that it was beginning to seep over the edges on to the grass.

"That's good," said the bear. "You're not leaving me any more! But what is wrong? Where is your happy and free bubbling sound?"

The stream was no longer trickling and bubbling along in its usual happy manner. It was still and sad. The bear was puzzled.

He tried jumping and splashing in the water. But the stream stayed still and sad.

He tried scooping up paws of lovely cool water to drink. But the stream was still and sad.

He tried lying down for a long bath. But the stream stayed still and sad.

The bear climbed out of the stream and sat sadly on the grassy bank.

An owl looked down from a tree at the bear.

"What's up, bear?" he hooted.

The bear wiped the tears from his eyes.

"The stream was leaving me. I tried to stop it because it's my friend and I don't want it to leave me. But I've just made everything worse. I've made the stream sad too."

The owl looked at the dam with his big round eyes.

"Move the stones and the rocks and the leaves and the sticky mud!" said the owl. "And then the stream will be happy again and so will you."

"But I don't understand," said the bear. "If I do that the stream will leave me."

"Just try it and see," said the owl.

So the bear moved the stones and the rocks and the leaves and the sticky mud and the water whooshed through and away. For a few minutes it bubbled happily and freely.

"Thank you for letting me go bear!" it said. "You've been the best friend. Now I can be happy and free again!"

But then it stopped. Suddenly there was no more water to trickle along.

"Follow me!" said the owl and flew along to where the last of the stream water was disappearing.

The bear followed. They reached the point where the stream joined a river.

"Look across there!" said the owl.

The bear looked down the river. He heard a rushing, gushing sound and hurried to see what it was.

"It's a beautiful waterfall!" said the bear.

"And your stream is part of it," said the owl.

It was true. The stream had finished with being a stream. It had joined the river. And now it was rushing and gushing over the waterfall with the rest of the river water.

The bear smiled.

"So it is!" he said. "And it sounds free and happy again. I was wrong to not let it go. This was where it needed to be. Good-bye little stream. I'll always know you're free and happy in the waterfall."

The bear turned back to the forest. He no longer felt sad. He would miss the stream, but he was glad he had let it go so that it could be free and happy.

A Heavy Load

A boy set off one day on a long journey. He was going to live in another town which was a long, long way away. He knew that it would take many hours to reach the town and the only way to get there was to walk.

Putting on his comfy walking shoes and carrying a light bag over his shoulder he set off. In the small bag he had everything he needed for the journey.

"Good luck in your new home!" called his friends.

It was a bright sunny day and after a few hours of walking the boy saw a small mouse sitting at the side of the path.

"Hello!" said the mouse. "Where are you going?"

"I'm walking to the new town to live there instead," said the boy.

"Really?" said the mouse. "Well, that's where I'm going as well!"

The boy looked at the tiny mouse and thought about the long journey ahead.

"Then let me help you, mouse!" he said. And before the mouse could reply he picked it up and sat it on his shoulder.

An hour later the boy met a duck. It had flown down from the sky and settled on the edge of a pond at the side of the path.

"Hello!" said the duck. "Where are you going?"

"I'm walking to the new town to live there instead," said the boy. "The mouse wants to go too, so I'm carrying him."

"Really?" said the duck. "Well, that's where I'm going as well!"

The boy looked at the duck and thought about the long journey ahead.

"Then let me help you, duck!" he said. And before the duck could reply he picked it up and sat it on his other shoulder.

An hour later the boy, with the mouse on one shoulder, the duck on the other and his bag on his back, met a dog. It was dozing in the sun at the side of the path.

"Hello!" said the dog. "Where are you going?"

The boy told the dog about his journey to the new town. "The mouse and the duck want to go too, so I'm carrying them."

"Really?" said the dog. "What a coincidence! That's where I'm going as well!"

The boy looked at the dog and thought about the long journey ahead.

"Then let me help you, dog!" he said. And before the dog could reply he picked it up and tucked it under one arm.

It was difficult carrying so much, but the boy carried on. After another hour he met a piglet.

"Hello!" said the piglet. "Where are you going?"

"I'm walking to the new town to live there instead," said the boy, staggering under the weight of his heavy load. "The mouse, the duck and the dog want to go too, so I'm carrying them."

"Are you?" said the piglet. "That's interesting. I'm on my way to the new town too."

The boy looked at the piglet. He sighed, but he said:

"Then let me help you!" and before the piglet could object he'd lifted it up and tucked it under his other arm.

And on he staggered. After another hour he met a girl. She was carrying a large parcel. She looked at the boy in astonishment.

"Where are you going?" she gasped. "How can you carry so much?"

Well, the boy explained about his journey and how he was carrying the mouse and the duck and the dog and the pig because they wanted to go too. And the girl said:

"Really? I'm about to post my parcel to the new town."

The boy looked at the parcel.

"Then let me help!" he said and, before the girl could say anything else, he took the parcel and managed to get it into the bag on his back without dropping anyone.

Now it was even more difficult to walk carrying so much. The boy had to walk very slowly now and his shoulders and back started to ache. The journey was much harder than he had thought it would be.

By the evening the boy was almost too tired to go any further and he was starting to feel fed up.

"If I wasn't carrying so much I'd be there by now!" he grumbled to himself.

"What's up?" said the mouse and the duck and the dog and the piglet.

"The journey is too difficult!" the boy said. But he didn't put the mouse and the duck and dog or the piglet down.

After another hour he met a man with a horse. They were resting in a field at the side of the path. The man looked at the boy and shook his head.

"That's no way to travel!" he said wisely. "You are carrying far too much!"

"Tell me about it!" said the boy. "I'm so tired and I ache all over."

The man felt sorry for the boy and he wanted to help.

"Here!" he offered. "Take my horse. That will make your journey easier."

And he walked off leaving his horse with the boy.

The boy looked at the horse and the horse looked at the boy. Because his hands were full, the boy took the horse's reins in his teeth and walked on and so the horse walked beside him.

On they walked. All evening. All night and on into the next morning. At last they were nearly at the new town. But the boy simply couldn't go any further. He stopped and sat down at the side of the path, too sore and exhausted to go any further. He began to wish he had never set off. And he began to sob.

"What's up?" said a voice. The boy looked up and saw a group of people from the new town had gathered around him. "And why are you carrying that heavy load?"

"I was trying to get to the new town," said the boy. "On my way I met the mouse and the duck and the dog and the piglet and the horse and a girl with a parcel and so…"

But he stopped because the group of people were laughing. Then they gently lifted the mouse from his shoulder and the duck from his other shoulder and the dog and the pig from under his arms. Then they removed the parcel from his bag.

"They would all have got there by themselves in their own way," said one person.

"You didn't need to carry them all," said another. "Whatever made you think you had to carry other people's loads?"

The boy watched in astonishment as the mouse and the duck and the dog and the piglet hurried on towards the new town all by themselves. And a passing parcel delivery man stopped to collect the parcel.

"And I guess a kind person gave you the horse so you could ride on it!" said someone else.

The horse swished his tail. That *had* been the idea.

"Oh," said the boy, wiping his eyes. "I was so busy carrying everyone who didn't need carrying that I didn't realise."

Then he too laughed and got to his feet. He felt so much lighter with just his own bag.

"Come on in!" said the crowd. "Welcome to our town!"

The boy hurried after his new friends. Walking alongside them he carried nothing but his own light bag. He was so relieved and so glad to have arrived. If only, he thought, he had realised that he hadn't needed to carry everyone else who was going there too. His journey would have been so much easier.

The Flower

THERE was once a girl who loved flowers. She loved them so much that she used to talk to them and imagined that they could hear and understand her!

"Hello, tiny brand new plant!" she would say to any brand new green shoot that she saw growing in her friends' gardens. "Grow big and strong and beautiful!"

And the brand new tiny plants always did. One day her friends, who knew how much she loved plants, gave her a special plant in a small pot. It was a tiny baby plant and hadn't yet flowered.

"This is just for you!" they said. "Now take care of it and watch it grow!"

The girl had never been given such a lovely gift before. She was very grateful, but it was an unusual flower and she was worried that she might not be able to look after it. How much water should it have? How much light? How much sun? Did it need to be indoors or out? Would the wind and rain harm it? She placed it indoors on a window ledge where she could see it and it would be safe and decided she would check every day to see how it was growing.

One day, as she was checking, she noticed that the special flower was not growing. While other people's plants seemed to grow strong green stems and buds that opened, this one looked pale and sickly. Its stem was thin and brown and the bud was stuck closed and hidden under a limp leaf.

"Oh dear!" said the girl. "Whatever is wrong? Why don't you want to grow big and strong and beautiful like other plants?"

She moved the sickly plant away from the window ledge and placed it on the table instead.

"There!" she encouraged it. "That should be better for you!"

But the next day, when she looked, the little bud had closed more tightly and the stem was still thin and brown.

She wondered if maybe she was watering it too much so she tried not watering it.

"Maybe that will be better for you!" she encouraged. "Perhaps that will help you grow!"

But the next day, when she looked, the plant had only grown another limp leaf, which covered the bud so that it was even more hidden.

The girl was puzzled. She had never seen a plant like this before. Surely it should be blooming and bursting out of its pot and ready for the big garden. But her one little plant wasn't growing properly at all.

She became more and more worried. What would her friends say if they saw it? She decided to hide the plant and put it in a warm cupboard in the bathroom. Perhaps it would prefer it in there anyway.

A few days later she remembered the plant in the cupboard and decided to take a look. But when she saw it she gasped in alarm.

"What has happened to you?" she cried. "I've kept you safe and warm and sheltered and you're still not growing!"

It was true. The little bud was still tightly shut, the leaves were still limp and the stem still brown.

"Perhaps you're still not warm enough!" she wondered and wrapped a small blanket around the pot. Then she put it back in the cupboard.

From then on the girl checked on the little plant every day. But every day the little plant looked more and more pale and sad and every day the girl grew more sad because of this.

"How's your plant?" her friends asked her one day.

But the girl was too upset to tell the truth and pretended that everything was well.

She kept the plant hidden and checked every day giving it a little water. But nothing ever changed. The little bud stayed tightly closed and the girl stayed unhappy because of this. She worried about the plant and she worried so much that she found she couldn't do anything else.

One day she had become so sad that her friends became concerned about her.

"Whatever is wrong?" they asked.

The girl started to cry and showed them the plant in the cupboard.

"I've kept it safe and warm and sheltered!" she sobbed. "But it's too scared to grow! It's going to be like this for ever!"

"Of course it's not!" said her friends. They carefully picked up the pot and took it out of the cupboard. "Plants have to have what they need to grow big and strong and beautiful. Once they have what they need then they can become what they're meant to be."

The girl was puzzled, but she dried her eyes and watched as her friends carried the little flower outside into the sunshine. They placed it in a bright sunny spot next to some other flowers and gave it some extra water.

The sun shone down on the little plant and warmed the soil around it. The bud turned slightly towards the light. A shower of rain fell and washed the pale leaves and soaked into the plant pot. After a few days the girl noticed that the bud was fatter and was starting to open. The leaves looked glossy and the stem had started to turn a green colour.

The girl was thrilled and the next time her friends came round she showed them the little plant.

"You were right!" she said. "I was so scared it wouldn't be safe and I'd kept it away from the sun and the air and the rain, but that meant it didn't grow."

As the days went by, the bud opened fully and became a beautiful flower. It grew stronger and bigger and eventually the girl had to remove it from the pot and plant it in the garden soil next to the other flowers. Then, the little plant that had been such a special gift, grew even taller and stronger.

Jack and the Rucksack

JACK carried a big rucksack around with him all the time. Day and night, at home, at school, at his friends' houses, out at the park, on holiday, everywhere. Wherever he went he carried the huge rucksack with him. He even took it to bed with him.

"Whatever have you got in that huge heavy bag?" people would ask him.

"I don't know!" Jack would answer. It was true! He didn't know. Most of the things he had put in the rucksack had been there a long time. He never took anything out of the bag and he never looked inside it. So he couldn't remember what was in there.

One day Jack's teacher told her class that there was going to be a spelling test at the end of the week. Jack didn't like spelling tests much. Last time he only got five spellings out of ten right. He started to worry about the spelling test.

"What's the matter?" his sister asked that evening at home.

The boy didn't tell his sister how much he was worried about the test.

"Nothing really," he said instead.

And suddenly the rucksack on his back got a bit heavier.

The next week some children in Jack's class started laughing at him because he'd forgotten his PE kit and had to do PE in some spare school shorts which were far too big. Jack didn't like being laughed at.

"Don't take any notice of them!" said his friends.

But Jack couldn't help feeling sad because people had laughed at him. He said nothing though. And suddenly the rucksack on his back got a bit heavier again.

Another day someone stole his best pencil case from his book bag. It was the one he'd had for his birthday. He was really annoyed and angry that someone should take it.

"What's up?" said his dad that night. "You look very cross. What's happened?"

"Nothing really!" said Jack.

"You really shouldn't walk around with that bag all the time!" Dad went on. "You're not going to take it with you tomorrow when we go to visit Grandad, are you?"

Grandad was poorly in hospital. But he loved having visitors. They cheered him up. But he too thought it was strange that Jack carried that bag everywhere he went.

The next day when Jack, his sister and his mum and dad went to visit Grandad he took the bag with him as usual. Grandad didn't look very well at all. He was too tired to talk or even sit up in bed.

Jack was worried. Was his grandad ever going to get better? A big lump of a sob formed in his chest.

His mum gave him a big hug.

"You know, Grandad has had a very good life and he is being well looked after here," she said.

But this didn't make Jack feel better. He said nothing.

And suddenly the rucksack on his back got even heavier.

And so it went on. Every now and then something would happen that made Jack feel sad or worried or angry. And the rucksack got even heavier. Whatever it was inside was getting bigger and bigger and heavier and heavier. There could hardly be any more room left inside it. It started to bulge and the zip looked as though it would burst.

Then finally, one day, IT HAPPENED.

Jack was cycling home from the park when he went over a big bump on the cycle track. His bike wobbled and tipped sideways and he fell heavily on the ground hitting his elbow. Jack couldn't move his arm and it was so painful that Mum and Dad had to take him to the hospital to get it checked out. At the hospital the doctors did x-rays and put Jack's broken arm in a plaster.

Jack was upset and annoyed. His arm hurt and now he wouldn't be able to cycle or play games properly or anything. This was too much. Suddenly with a big BANG the rucksack on his back burst and exploded and a big whoosh of air came out like a giant balloon exploding. Jack cried and sobbed and yelled and howled. No one had ever heard him make so much noise.

Then he told his mum and dad and the doctor how fed up he was, how upset and how angry and worried. He told them all about how much he hated spelling tests and how worried he was about the kids at school who laughed at him, how upset he was about having his favourite pencil case stolen and how worried about Grandad he was. His mum pulled the remains of the rucksack off his shoulders and put it on the floor.

"It's alright to get upset and angry!" she said. "You don't need to stuff everything away about how you feel and never tell anyone! It's important to say how you feel. If you don't then everything will build up inside you getting bigger and bigger. It makes you feel worse. But Jack, everyone who loves you cares and wants to help."

Jack had never thought about this before. Whenever something sad or worrying had happened he had just kept it to himself and not said how it made him feel. That was why he had got so weighed down with everything.

Jack stopped crying and hugged his mum and smiled. She was right. It did feel better to say how you felt and people did care. People did want to help.

It took a while for Jack's arm to mend, but it did and he was soon back to riding his bicycle and doing everything he usually did again. But better than that, he had decided not to carry the rucksack around with him any more. From then on if he felt sad or upset or annoyed or worried he told someone. Sometimes he talked to his friends. Sometimes he talked to his mum or dad or his sister. He didn't feel like he was carrying a big rucksack around with all his hidden feelings in any more. It was good knowing that even if sad or difficult things happened there was always someone to tell and that could help a lot.

The Wish

THERE was once a wishing well that contained all the wishes anyone could ever think to wish. People came from all over the world to drop coins into the well and make their wishes. There were wishes for people who wanted pets, wishes for people who wanted new things, wishes for people who wanted holidays, wishes for people who wanted to get better when they were ill or who wanted someone they knew who was ill to get better. There were wishes for lonely people who wanted friends, wishes for children who didn't have parents and wishes for people who needed somewhere to live.

Every time someone dropped a coin into the water and said: "I wish for…" the correct wish floated up from the well and set about helping the person make their own wish come true.

As you can imagine all of the wishes down in the well were kept very busy. There was hardly an hour that went by when they weren't hard at work.

But there was one wish that no one ever wished for. That little wish sat patiently and alone day after day, week after week, month after month and year after year waiting for someone to wish for her. But no one ever did.

"Obviously no one wants you!" said the other wishes. "What's the good of a wish that no one wants? Perhaps you should change and be a different wish!"

But the little wish knew she couldn't change. She could only be herself.

It was sad and lonely watching all the other wishes rushing around looking wanted and important and making lots of people happy.

She asked the well what she should do.

"No one wants me!" she said to the well. "Why am I here when I'm so different and alone? I'm the only one left out. It isn't fair!"

The well felt sorry for the little wish. But he couldn't change anything for her.

"You need to believe in yourself!" he said. "The other wishes are wrong when they say no one wants you. Don't listen to them. Things will change for you one day. Just wait and see! One day you will believe it."

The little wish hoped the well was right. She waited alone and feeling different for a long time. She tried hard not to feel sad and she tried hard to believe in herself.

While all the other wishes hurried about their work the little wish spent her time listening to the people who came to the well. She noticed how sad some were. She noticed that some had big hopes and some had no hope.

Then one day she noticed a boy standing by the well. He was looking with sad eyes down at the water below and at all the coins others had tossed in to make their wishes. But this boy didn't throw a coin into the water and make a wish. He waited a while and then walked sadly away.

The next day the boy came back to the well. Once again he looked sadly at the deep water and then walked away again.

The little wish was puzzled.

"What's wrong with the little boy?" she asked the well.

"Ah!" said the well. "People like that boy do come here sometimes. But they don't make their wish!"

"But why not?" said the little wish. "He looks as though he must have a wish!"

"He does!" said the well. "But he doesn't make the wish because he doesn't believe in himself. Because he doesn't believe in himself he doesn't think his wish will work."

The little wish gasped. A ripple of excitement bubbled up inside her.

"He doesn't believe in himself!" she repeated. "He doesn't believe in himself and so he doesn't think his wish will work. He doesn't think anything can change!"

For some reason the little wish found herself looking forward to the boy's visits. Every time he gazed longingly into the water the little wish called out to him.

"Just wish it! Just wish it! You can! You can! You can believe in yourself! You can make your own wish come true!"

And it was almost as if the boy had heard her because he said out loud to himself:

"No! No one wants me! I'm different and left out! It will always be like this!"

And the little wish called out louder:

"Just wish it! Just wish it! You can! You can! You can believe in yourself!"

And so it went on. The little wish soon forgot about being sad and lonely herself. She was too busy thinking about the little boy – she knew she could help him.

Then, one day when the boy visited the well, she noticed that he was holding a coin in his hand. He was still looking sad, but there was a glimmer of hope in his eyes. He stretched out his arm and held the coin between his thumb and one finger. The little wish was very excited.

"Just wish it! Just wish it!" she encouraged.

The boy took a deep breath and let go of the coin. As it tumbled and turned and dropped its way down to the water he spoke his wish out loud.

"I don't want to think I'm unwanted any more! I want to know I can have friends like everyone else!"

Suddenly the little wish felt that same ripple of excitement bubbling up inside her. It was her! It was her! She was the wish people needed when they needed to believe in themselves. She was the wish who could change things for the little boy.

With a whoosh she rushed up from the well and, invisible as wishes are, she wrapped herself around the little boy in a warm and encouraging hug. Then she looked around. She would get busy at once making the boy's wish come true. She noticed some other children playing nearby.

The boy sighed. Somehow he felt different. He wasn't sure why, but he didn't feel sad and alone any more. He had a warm and hopeful feeling. He looked at the other children playing nearby. Usually he didn't play with other children. Not because he didn't want to, but because once some other children had unkindly told him they didn't want him playing with them and from then on he had always believed he was different and unwanted. He had felt so lonely and unwanted for so long. But now he hurried over to these other children with a big smile on his face.

"Hello!" they said, noticing how friendly he looked. "D'you want to play?"

The boy was astonished. They wanted him to play and be his friend! His wish was beginning to come true already. That little voice he'd kept hearing in his head was right. It had told him to believe in himself and that things would get better.

The little wish watched in delight as the boy began playing with his new friends. Just like her he had needed to believe in himself. He no longer believed the unkind lies that told him he was different or unwanted. Now, instead, he knew he was as okay as anyone else. And so he began to feel stronger and happier and could make his own wishes come true.

Broken

EMMA didn't really like school. The only thing she liked about it was art. There were only two art lessons a week. Emma would have liked art all day every day instead of boring maths and English and other dull stuff.

Everyone said that Emma took after her Gran because her Gran had been 'creative'. Emma wasn't sure what that meant, but remembered that Gran had been amazing at making jewellery and clever things out of beads and glass and clay. On her last birthday she'd given Emma a pretty box for keeping special things in. It was very delicate and had an orange and yellow lid made out of glass and was decorated with gold and white beads. Emma loved it because Gran had made it and it was perfect for keeping things like make-up and earrings in. But more than that it was the last thing Gran had made before she got ill and had died.

So when Emma came home from school one day and said that her art homework was to make a picture that showed a special present Dad said:

"Well, that's easy! You can draw that lovely box Gran made you, Emma!"

Emma thought about this. It was true it was a special present. But could she draw it? Could she paint in all the colours so that the box looked as beautiful in a picture as it was in real life? She wasn't sure.

All weekend Emma worked away at the picture. She placed the delicate glass box on the kitchen table next to her art book and paints and started sketching. It was hard work getting it just right, but eventually she managed it. She held her big art book up in front of her to take a good look.

"Hmm!" she said to herself. "I think it just needs a bit more gold paint here and…"

Reaching across the table for a smaller brush her sleeve caught the edge of the delicate box and before she knew it…

CRASH!

"Ahhhhhh!" Emma screamed as the beautiful gift fell off the edge of the table, landed on the hard floor and smashed into tiny pieces.

For a few seconds she stared in horror and disbelief. Then she screamed and cried in panic.

Emma's mum and dad rushed into the kitchen and gasped when they saw what had happened.

"It's broken!" Emma wailed. "Look what's happened! I've lost my beautiful box!"

Emma left her picture unfinished. She was too upset to finish it. Her special box was gone. Broken. Destroyed.

Dad brushed up all the pieces and tipped them into a small cardboard box, but Emma wouldn't let him put it out in the recycling bin. She took the box and went to her room and stayed there for the rest of the weekend.

After that Emma went off art as well. Now there was nothing she liked about school.

"If it wasn't for that picture I'd been trying to do, then the box would never have got broken!" she said. "I'm never going to draw anything again!"

And for a long time she didn't. And for a long time she felt miserable. In her room she kept the box of broken pieces. Sometimes she looked at them and sighed.

"If only I could mend it," she would think to herself. "If only I could turn all the broken bits back into my beautiful box again!"

But, of course, that wasn't possible. So Emma went on feeling miserable every time she thought about it.

Months went by and then one day Mum was having a clear out. She wanted to take some things they didn't want any more to the charity shop. She was putting everything into a large bag.

"What about those jeans and t-shirts that don't fit you any more?" she asked Emma.

"Sure!" said Emma. "You can take those. And you can have these old books. They're for little kids. I'm too old for them."

Mum waited in Emma's room while Emma grabbed all the stuff and put it in the charity bag. Then Mum spotted the box of broken pieces.

"You've still got that?" she said in astonishment.

Emma sighed. "Well, I keep wishing I could think of a way to mend it," she said. "It'll never be the same though!"

Mum thought for a minute.

"Mmm!" she said. "You're right. It won't ever be the same. It can't be your special box again even though you loved it so much. But… well, maybe it's time to give up holding on to all the broken pieces. Maybe there is something we could do instead."

Ten minutes later Emma and Mum were sitting at the kitchen table. They'd tipped all the broken pieces out of the box and for a moment they stared at the pattern this made on the table. Emma laughed.

"It looks like…!" she said.

"It does!" Mum agreed. She pushed some of the pieces together and Emma rearranged some of the dark beads. After a while they had a real picture made from the broken pieces.

"I've got an idea!" Emma jumped up and fetched her art book. She opened it at a page at the back. It showed blue sky, sunshine, white clouds, butterflies, green grass and tiny flowers. It was one of Emma's best pictures.

Carefully she transferred the tiny broken pieces from the table onto the middle of her picture. It took a while, but eventually all of the pieces were in place.

"What do you think?" she asked.

"Well, who would have thought it!" said Mum. "That is astonishing. And very clever!"

Next Emma got some glue and together they fixed each tiny piece in place.

"They need to be sitting on something," Emma said when the gluing was all done. "They need a tree branch to sit on or something. Or maybe just a…"

Emma carefully drew a pencil line from one side of the page to the other so that it went under the three sparkling glass and bead owls.

A few hours later, once the picture had dried, they carefully removed it from Emma's art book.

It was Dad's idea to put the picture in a frame and then they hung the frame in Emma's room.

Emma was thrilled. She might not have her special box any more, but this was good. She loved it. She would never have thought it was possible for something new and good to come out of something that had been so broken.

Somehow she knew Gran would have loved it too.

This book and those below are part of the award winning Story Therapy® Series from Strawberry Jam Books:

Stories for Feelings for Children: Illustrated Edition

The Forever Tree

Just Be with Bizzy Bee

Little Acorn and the Great Big Happy Hug

Imagine! cd and audio – interactive narratives with musical backgrounds

For details and all titles, games and resources see:

www.storytherapyresources.co.uk

www.ingramcontent.com/pod-product-compliance
Lightning Source LLC
LaVergne TN
LVHW042004060526
838200LV00041B/1870